Life of a Star

BY STACIA DEUTSCH AND RHODY COHON

Table of Contents

Pictures To Think About

carbon
and
oxygen

helium fusing

shell

Words To Think About

Characteristics

group of stars, gas, and dust

held together by gravity

?

galaxy

What do you think the word galaxy means?

Examples

Milky Way Galaxy

Bear Paw Galaxy

?

asteroid

What do you think the word asteroid means?

Greek: *aster* (star)

Greek: *eidos* (a form)

Read for More Clues

asteroid, page 9
galaxy, page 3
spectral class, page 4

spectral class

What do you think the term **spectral class** means?

What is **spectral class**?

What is **spectral class** based on?

way to sort stars	?	seven types in all

color	?	temperature

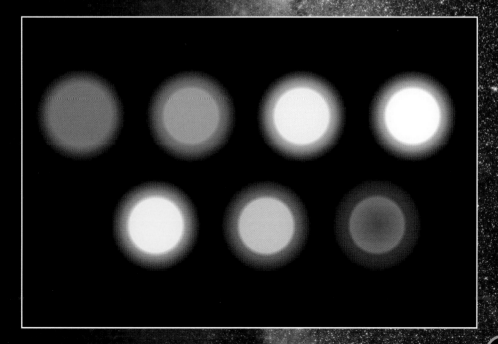

Introduction

Look at the night sky. How many stars can you see? Long ago, people watched these twinkling white dots. People used the stars to guide them when they went places.

Back then, the stars were a mystery. People did not know what stars were. They did not know how stars got in the sky. Some people made up stories, or myths, about the stars. The myths told how the stars got in the sky. Some myths said that the stars were once people. Other myths said that the stars were once gods and goddesses.

Over time, people invented tools like telescopes to see stars. These tools let scientists see stars better. **Astronomers** (uh-STRAH-nuh-merz) are scientists who study stars and planets. Today, we know that a star is a giant ball of gas. We also know that stars give off light and heat.

Constellations are ▶ groupings of stars. The groups form shapes and patterns.

Stars gather in groups. The groups are called **galaxies** (GA-luk-seez). What brings stars together in groups? The answer is **gravity** (GRA-vih-tee). Gravity is a force that pulls things together.

A galaxy can have millions of stars. The universe has more than a trillion galaxies.

This book is about the life cycle of a star. First, you will learn how stars form. Then you will learn how stars change. You will read about a star's **main sequence** (MANE SEE-kwens) stage. Then you will see how stars fade from the sky.

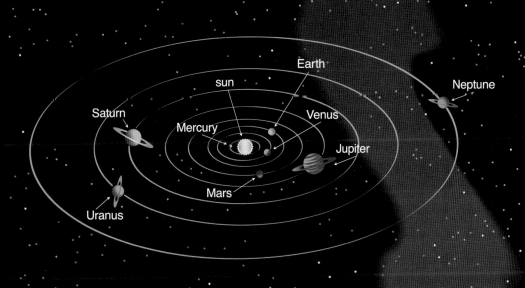

Earth
sun
Neptune
Saturn
Venus
Mercury
Jupiter
Mars
Uranus

▲ **Our solar system is comprised of everything that orbits the sun, including planets.**

Birth of a Star

The stars in the sky seem more or less the same. Look more closely and you will see different types of stars.

Spectral Classes

Scientists divide stars into different groups. Each group is called a **spectral class** (SPEK-trul KLAS). To sort stars, scientists look at their temperatures. They also look at how quickly a star uses its fuel. Finally, a star is also sorted by the color it burns. These classes are labeled O, B, A, F, G, K, and M.

It's a Fact

Stars seem to twinkle. This is because starlight must pass through layers of moving air in Earth's atmosphere. The air bends the light back and forth.

▼ Stars are classified by temperature, and by weight, radius, and luminosity (loo-mih-NAH-sih-tee), or how much light the star gives off.

Spectral Class Types for Stars

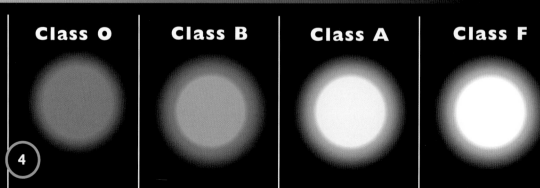

Class O   Class B   Class A   Class F

Class O blue stars have high temperatures. They burn fuel quickly. They also have the shortest life. They last from 10,000 to 100,000 years.

Medium yellow stars are class G. They burn fuel slower, so they live longer. They last about ten billion years.

The coolest, slowest-burning red stars are class M. Red stars are the most common type of star. We rarely see them, though. This is because they are so small compared to other stars. These stars burn their fuel very slowly, which allows them to live trillions of years.

▼ Our sun is a class G yellow star.

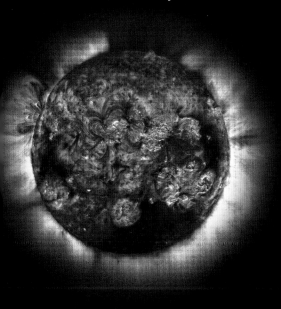

Everyday Science

Have you ever thought about counting the stars you see in the night sky? It may seem that there are too many to count. Actually, the unaided eye can see only a few thousand stars.

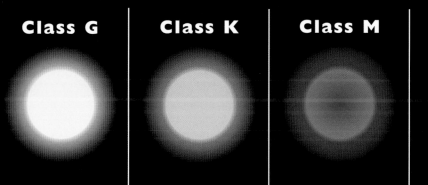

Class G **Class K** **Class M**

Nebulas, Where Stars Are Born

All stars are born in the same way. All stars begin in a **nebula** (NEH-byuh-luh). This is a thick cloud of gas and dust in space. Nebulas contain mainly hydrogen gas. They also have a small amount of helium gas.

There are different types of nebulas. Some nebulas give off light. Some nebulas reflect the light of stars around them. A planetary nebula forms when a small star dies and sheds its outer layers. A dark nebula has so much dust and gas that it blocks out all light around it.

Dark nebula clouds are often very large. They can span across many millions of miles. Scientists believe that stars are born inside these dark nebulas.

Careers
Astronomers

Astronomers observe the skies through telescopes. They use modern technology, such as computers and satellite pictures, to make discoveries. To prepare for their career, astronomers must go to college. They take many science and math courses. They also take astronomy courses.

The Horsehead Nebula ▶ is a dark nebula from the constellation Orion.

Inside the dark nebula, gas and dust stick together and form clumps. A large clump has more gravity. This gravity pulls more gas and dust to the clump. The clump increases in size and mass. Mass is the amount of matter that something contains.

The gravity continues to pull the dust and gas particles very close together. Sometimes a nearby star explodes. The explosion sends out shock waves. The shock waves can push the gas and dust particles even closer together.

The thickly packed gas and dust inside the clump create a very hot, dense core, or center. In time, the nebula collapses. This is the beginning of a new star.

▲ Some astronomers think the gas and other materials in the Witchhead Reflection Nebula look like the face of a witch.

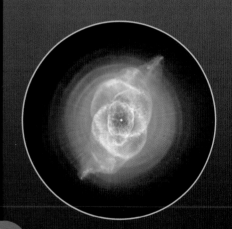

▲ Planetary nebulas emerge at the end of one star's life and mark the beginning for another.

Math Matters The brightness of an object in the night sky is called its apparent magnitude. This measure depends on two things. The first is how brightly the object actually shines. The second is its distance from Earth. Ancient Greeks divided the visible stars into six magnitudes. The brightest stars were said to be of first magnitude. The faintest were of sixth magnitude. Astronomers today still figure out a star's brightness based on this ancient principle.

As the nebula collapses, its core begins to rotate, or spin. The dust begins to flatten out into a disk. This **protoplanetary** (proh-toh-PLA-neh-tair-ee) **disk** spins for about another ten million years. Then the disk disappears.

We do not know why the disk disappears. Astronomers have two ideas. One idea is that after a while, the disk does not give off enough radiation for us to measure. Radiation is the sending out of light rays and heat rays. The disk might still be there, but we can no longer see it.

Historical Perspective

In 1924, Edwin Hubble found a winking star in the Andromeda Galaxy. He showed that this star was outside the Milky Way. Until that time, people believed that the Milky Way was the only galaxy in the universe. The Hubble Space Telescope is named for this astronomer.

 **POINT**

Make Connections

The sun is our most familiar star. Write three things you already knew about the sun. Then write three things you learned about the sun from *Life of a Star*.

The second idea is that pieces of the disk become new planets. Or the pieces might become **asteroids** (AS-tuh-roidz). Asteroids are large rocky objects that orbit the sun.

When the protoplanetary disk disappears, it is easy to see what it leaves behind. The central core is what will soon become a star.

Everyday Science

Many meteoroids are pieces of asteroids broken off by collisions. When a meteoroid comes too close to Earth, it burns up in our atmosphere. You may have seen a streak of light across the night sky. People sometimes call the streak a shooting star. The actual name for this streak is a meteor.

▲ A star is forming inside the Eagle Nebula.

Protostar

In time, the central core becomes so hot and dense that light can no longer pass through it. The star's radiation no longer causes the mass to change. During this phase, a new star is called a **protostar** (PROH-toh-star).

Over time, the outer layers of the protostar's gas get larger and heavier. Gravity from the layers of gas and the core pull at each other. This puts pressure on the gas in the core. As a result, the gases in the core grow even hotter and more dense. Atoms move faster and crash into one another. The pressure squeezes the atoms of hydrogen gas together. The atoms begin to stick to one another. They fuse to form helium atoms. This process is called **nuclear fusion** (NOO-klee-er FYOO-zhun).

Nuclear fusion releases vast amounts of energy. The energy creates huge jets of gas, called **bipolar outflow**. These gas jets break apart the rest of the dusty protoplanetary disk.

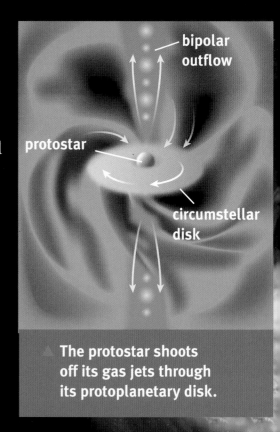

bipolar outflow

protostar

circumstellar disk

The protostar shoots off its gas jets through its protoplanetary disk.

Nuclear fusion is the key to a star's birth. After a few million years, the main part of the disk will disappear. The young star in the middle of the cloud can now be seen. The star's size depends on how much gas and dust it gathered during formation.

It may take forty million years for a star to be born. For a star, this is not a long time. The next stage in a star's life cycle lasts even longer.

▲ Sometimes stars form in clusters. This is because some nebulas have multiple areas of clumping.

▲ This is a brand-new sun-sized star called a T-Tauri star. It's named after a star in the constellation of Taurus. So far, astronomers have observed more than 500 T-Tauri stars.

Main Sequence of a Star

A star's mass decides whether it moves on to the next stage. Mass also controls the length of a star's life and how it will die. For example, not all protostars go on to become true stars. A protostar cannot begin nuclear fusion without enough mass or heat. Without nuclear fusion, a protostar becomes a brown dwarf star. This star is a cold mass of debris. It is not hot enough or heavy enough to make its own light.

Other protostars are large enough and hot enough to enter the next stage. This is known as the main sequence stage. During this stage, nuclear fusion happens continuously in a star's core. The star gives off rays of light and energy. A star remains in this stage for most of its life.

Nuclear fusion creates ▶ very light, nonelectric charges called neutrinos. By studying these neutrinos, scientists learn about fusion inside the stars.

▲ Is this a picture of a brown dwarf? Scientists are unsure. It's hard to spot a brown dwarf. It often looks the same as a large planet.

Parts of a Star

The sun is a medium-sized star. Astronomers study the sun because it is only about 93 million miles (150 million kilometers) away. Other main sequence stars are billions or even trillions of miles away and hard to see clearly.

The sun has the same parts as all main sequence stars. All main sequence stars have a:

Core: This is where the sun makes its energy.

Radiative Zone: This zone is outside the core. Here, energy moves in the form of photons (FOH-tahnz). Photons are a type of radiation.

▲ Solar flares are sudden, violent explosions on the sun. Over time, a solar flare's radiation and particles reach Earth's magnetic field. Then the particles can disrupt electrical systems, such as power grids, on Earth.

Convective Zone: This layer is less dense and cooler than the radiative zone. Here, hot gas currents from the radiative zone carry photons toward the surface. These currents make the surface look like it is boiling.

Photosphere: This is the star's atmosphere. It emits light.

Chromosphere: A hot region where shock waves from the photosphere produce millions of tiny spikes of hot gas called **spicules** (SPIH-kyoolz).

Corona: This is the layer of gases around the star. It is much hotter here than the core. The temperature of the corona averages 3.6 million degrees Fahrenheit (2 million degrees Celsius).

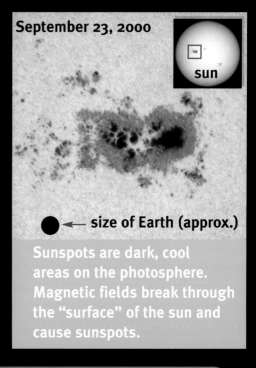

September 23, 2000

sun

← size of Earth (approx.)

Sunspots are dark, cool areas on the photosphere. Magnetic fields break through the "surface" of the sun and cause sunspots.

Historical Perspective

In 1543, Polish astronomer Nicolaus Copernicus (NIH-kuh-lus koh-PER-nih-kus) became the first to declare that Earth traveled around the sun. However, the Roman Catholic Church declared that the sun revolved around Earth. To disagree with a Church belief was a crime. In 1609, Italian Galileo Galilei (ga-lih-LAY-oh GA-lih-lee) built a telescope and observed the motions of planets in the solar system. He discovered that Copernicus was right. Galileo was arrested when he disagreed with the Church. He spent the rest of his life under house arrest.

How long a star remains in main sequence depends on its mass and amount of fuel. Very large stars are much hotter and brighter than smaller stars, like our sun. Yet stars with greater mass need more energy to stay in equilibrium. Very large stars burn much more quickly than medium and small stars. This means that the larger a star is, the shorter its life will be.

One of the most massive stars known today is Eta Carinae (AY-tuh kuh-RY-nuh). Eta Carinae is highly unstable. Chunks of the star's outer layers often blast off into space.

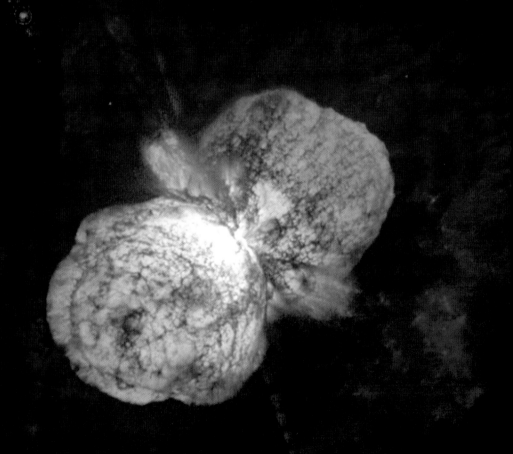

▲ In the mid-1800s, Eta Carinae was one of the brightest stars in the evening sky. Today, it cannot be seen without a telescope.

A star of this size will have a very short life. Astronomers predict that this star will live only one million years.

A star spends about ninety percent of its life in the main sequence stage. This can be millions or billions of years. Over time, a star runs out of fuel. When this happens, a star enters its next life stage.

Mass of the Sun	Luminosity of the Sun	Life Span of a Star
25M	200,000L	3e6 years*
15M	30,000L	15e6 years
3M	65L	500e6 years
1.5M	5L	3e9 years
1M	1L	10e9 years
0.8M	0.4L	13e9 years
0.4M	0.03L	200e9 years

*e = exponent

▲ Astronomers predict the length of a star's life by comparing it to the mass (M) and luminosity (L) of the sun.

Math Matters Scientists use a special measurement called a light-year for huge distances. A light-year is the distance that light rays travel in one year. That's equal to about 5.9 trillion miles (9.5 trillion kilometers). Astronomers need this large of a measurement since stars are so far away. For example, the distance between Earth and the next closest star after the sun, Proxima Centauri, is about 4.2 light-years.

Death of a Star

A star enters its final life stages as it runs out of fuel. Without fuel, a star cannot perform nuclear fusion as it once did. Its temperature begins to drop, and the star's gas cools. The star grows unbalanced. It loses its equilibrium. Gravity begins to make the star contract, or become smaller.

Red Giant Stage

The star keeps burning up its hydrogen. This leaves a core of helium. The core needs to get hotter to use the helium as its fuel. To create the necessary high temperature, the core begins to contract as well.

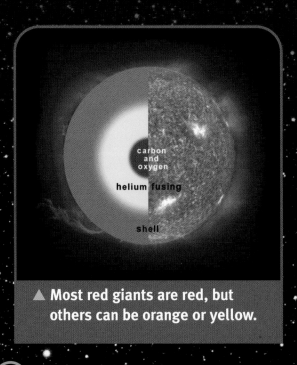

carbon and oxygen

helium fusing

shell

▲ Most red giants are red, but others can be orange or yellow.

▲ Aldebaran, a red giant, is one of the brightest stars in the night sky.

Part of the star's core becomes hot enough to begin nuclear fusion again. This time, the core turns helium into iron, carbon, nitrogen, and oxygen. The dying star gains energy once more.

Now the core burns hotter than during its main sequence. The outer parts of the star swell in an effort to release some of the heat. The star grows. But by the time the energy reaches the star's surface, it is weak and red-colored.

A medium or small star in this stage is called a red giant. A large star in this stage is called a red supergiant.

Some red giants may regain stability for a while. Then, they begin the red giant stage a second time. ▼

Someday our sun will also become a red giant. Scientists believe that the sun will not leave its main sequence for another five to seven billion years. So they look at other stars to learn about the red giant stage of life.

As a red giant uses up its fuel, it becomes unstable. It begins to slowly vibrate, or shake. Then, over many years, the vibrations grow faster. The vibrations push away the outer parts of the star.

In Their Own Words

"We find them smaller and fainter, in constantly increasing numbers, and we know that we are reaching into space, farther and farther, until, with the faintest nebulae that can be detected with the greatest telescopes, we arrive at the frontier of the known universe."

— Edwin Powell Hubble describing finding distant stars

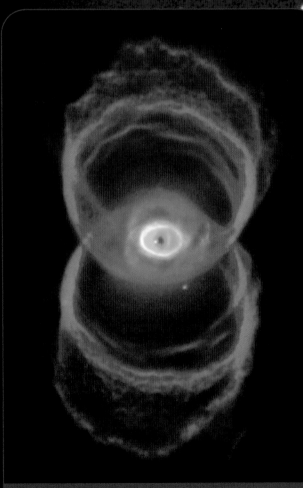

▲ The Hubble Space Telescope took this picture of an hourglass-shaped nebula surrounding a dying star.

Dust and gas form a shell around the dying star. This ring-shaped shell is a planetary nebula.

Planetary nebulas look like greenish planets. For this reason, an astronomer named Wilhelm Herschel called them planetary nebulas.

Planetary nebulas have very short lives. They last only about 10,000 years. About 1,500 planetary nebulas are known to exist in our galaxy.

▲ Studying planetary nebulas, such as the Egg Nebula, may help us understand how red giants turn into nebulas.

21

After a red giant has created a planetary nebula, only its core remains. The core stays inside the nebula. But it has used up all its fuel. It can no longer do nuclear fusion. The star then enters the next life stage. It is now a **white dwarf**.

White dwarf stars are ▶ formed when small or medium-sized stars die.

White Dwarfs and Black Dwarfs

Over the next billion years, a white dwarf's temperature slowly cools down. It emits very little light. Because of this, white dwarfs are very small and hard to detect. A white dwarf is only a fraction of its former weight.

It's a Fact

Some giants aren't red. They are blue. However, dying massive stars do not create blue giants. Blue giants are simply large stars that have a bluish color.

At first, white dwarfs are so hot that they still glow. But in time, white dwarfs cool to temperatures so low that they cannot be seen. Then they will be in their last life stage: a dead star. All that will remain is a black lump of carbon, known as a black dwarf.

We know of no black dwarfs in our universe. Scientists think none have been created yet. Scientists are trying to figure out how long it takes for a white dwarf to become a black dwarf. Knowing this may help them find out the age of our universe.

▲ Astronomers use X-ray satellite pictures
to find white dwarf stars.

23

Red Supergiants

Small- to medium-sized stars become red giants. But large dying stars become red supergiants.

Red supergiants begin to die like red giants do. Their gravity causes the outer layers to collapse inward. Then the matter reheats. Nuclear fusion begins again. The star swells and glows red.

Unlike red giants, red supergiants may have strong stellar winds. The outer layer is stable. But underneath it, hydrogen is actively fusing into helium. As go inward toward the core, the layers get hotter and more dens

Scientists think ▶ the red supergiant Betelgeuse will enter its final life stage soon, perhaps even in our lifetime.

Sometimes a red supergiant's core cools slightly. This makes the core contract. The surface of the star grows even hotter. The hot temperature makes the star glow blue. The star turns into a blue supergiant for a short time. Then, as the core heats up again, the outer surface cools. The star goes back to red.

Bright red supergiants live one million years or less. When one enters its final life stage, the star mostly burns carbon into iron. Then it will last only a short time longer.

Red supergiants do not become white dwarfs. They produce a huge stellar explosion called a **supernova** (soo-per-NOH-vuh).

▲ Many think this Anasazi pictograph is of the 1054 Crab Nebula supernova. It was drawn on a rock wall in Chaco Canyon, New Mexico.

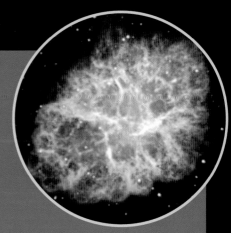

Eyewitness Account

On July 4, 1054, a Chinese stargazer wrote this about a new object in the sky: *"In the first year of the period Chih-ho, the fifth moon, the day chi-ch'ou, a guest star appeared. . . . After more than a year it gradually became invisible. . . ."* Scientists now know that this object was really a supernova. Sketches of this supernova appeared in ancient Anasazi drawings of the same period. Today, it's called the Crab Nebula.

▲ The Crab Nebula is the result of a supernova. It is about 6,000 light-years away.

25

Supernovas

A supernova is caused in the star's core. In the core, carbon is turned into iron. The iron is too heavy for fusion to continue. The core begins to take in energy rather than give it off. The core collapses. This collapse creates a huge amount of energy.

The energy is released as a very, very bright supernova. Supernovas blast gas and debris far into space. These bits may form a new nebula.

Neutron Stars, Pulsars, and Black Holes

The remains of a large supernova may form a neutron star. A neutron star has a very dense core. In the core, protons and electrons combine to form neutrons. This gives the star its name.

◀ The supernova 1987A exploded approximately 160,000 years ago. The light from it didn't reach Earth until February 23, 1987.

All neutron stars rotate, but some also "twinkle." Pulsars are spinning neutron stars. They give off radio waves, or pulses. Scientists use radio telescopes to record the pulses and study them. Pulsars also release jets of light, creating a twinkle effect.

In more massive stars, the outer layers collapse. Sometimes the inner core's gravity is so strong that the collapse crushes all matter. In these cases, the supernova creates a black hole. This is an area of space where gravity is so strong that nothing, not even light, can escape it.

In 2004, astronomers ▶ discovered a black hole in a far-off galaxy. They named it Q0906+6930.

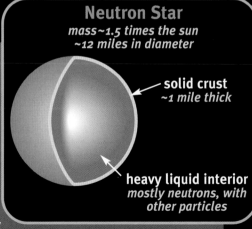

Neutron Star
mass~1.5 times the sun
~12 miles in diameter

solid crust
~1 mile thick

heavy liquid interior
mostly neutrons, with other particles

They Made a Difference

Astronomer Jocelyn Bell discovered the first pulsar in 1967. At first, she was confused by the fast and constant radio signal the spinning neutron star produced. She and her partner labeled the signal LGM, for Little Green Men. They thought that maybe the sound was coming from aliens!

▲ A newly born neutron star rotates very quickly, often several times per second.

Conclusion

Stars are an important part of our universe. They release light and heat far into space. Their gravity pulls other objects into orbit around them. This creates galaxies and solar systems.

Every living thing on Earth depends on a star, our sun. Our sun supplies Earth with light and heat. Without the sun, everything on Earth would die.

A star changes as it moves through its life cycle. A star is born in a nebula cloud. Then it enters the protostar stage. The protostar stage lasts only a few million years. Next, it becomes a main sequence star.

While in its main sequence, a star begins to shine. The star may live like this for many millions, perhaps even billions, of years.

Scientists think that ▶ typical galaxies contain between ten million and one trillion stars.

In time, the star will run out of fuel and begin to cool. A medium- to small-sized star will become a red giant. A large-mass star will become a red supergiant.

As a red giant uses up its final fuel, it sheds its outer layers. A planetary nebula forms around the dying star.

The dying star is now a white dwarf. Over time, white dwarfs cool. All that is left is a lifeless black dwarf.

Red supergiants do not become white dwarfs. Instead, they explode in a great burst called a supernova.

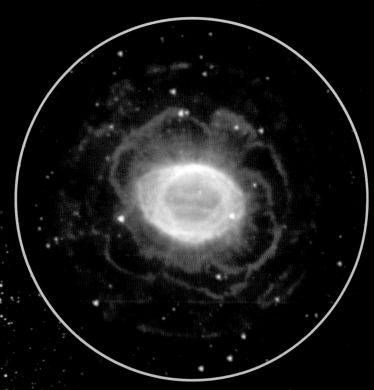

▲ There is a dying white dwarf star inside this Ring Nebula.

What remains after the supernova depends on the star's size. The supernova may create a neutron star or a pulsar. Sometimes it forms a black hole.

No matter how a star dies, space has a great recycling program. Dying stars toss away gas and matter. These eventually become nebulas again. New stars form in these nebulas.

We learn more about the stars every day. Modern telescopes and space exploration can show us many new things. But there is still much more to learn. The night sky still holds mysteries, just as it did for people long, long ago.

 **POINT**

Read More About It

Ask your teacher or librarian to help you find books and Internet sites about star myths. Choose your favorite story and retell it to a partner.

Life Cycle of Stars

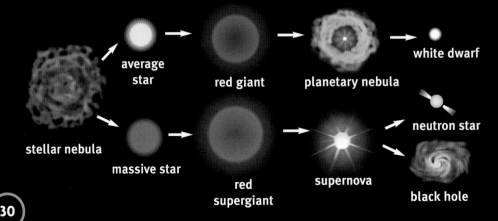

stellar nebula

average star

red giant

planetary nebula

white dwarf

massive star

red supergiant

supernova

neutron star

black hole

Glossary

asteroid	(AS-tuh-roid) a large, rocky object that travels through space (page 9)
astronomer	(uh-STRAH-nuh-mer) a scientist who studies the planets, objects, gas, and matter outside Earth's atmosphere (page 2)
bipolar outflow	(by-POH-ler OWT-floh) jets of gas that shoot away from a protostar (page 10)
galaxy	(GA-luk-see) a group of stars, gases, and dust in a given area held together by gravity (page 3)
gravity	(GRA-vih-tee) a force that attracts things to each other (page 3)
main sequence	(MANE SEE-kwens) the stage in which nuclear fusion happens in a star's core (page 3)
nebula	(NEH-byuh-luh) a thick cloud of space gas and dust (page 6)
nuclear fusion	(NOO-klee-er FYOO-zhun) the process by which atoms fuse to form new atoms and release heat and light energy (page 10)
protoplanetary disk	(proh-toh-PLA-neh-tair-ee DISK) a cloud of dust pushed away from a nebula when fusion begins (page 8)
protostar	(PROH-toh-star) the stage in a star's life before nuclear fusion begins (page 10)
spectral class	(SPEK-trul KLAS) a grouping of stars (page 4)
spicule	(SPIH-kyool) a tiny spike of hot gas from a star's chromosphere (page 15)
stable equilibrium	(STAY-bul ee-kwih-LIH-bree-um) a state where the gravitational pull inward and the gas pressure outward are in balance (page 13)
supernova	(soo-per-NOH-vuh) a huge explosion that occurs at the end of a super-massive star's life (page 25)
white dwarf	(WITE DWORF) the small, dense remains after a red giant star dies (page 22)

Index